# EAST OF NOWHERE

# EAST OF NOWHERE

## Larry Christianson

NORTH STAR PRESS OF ST. CLOUD, INC.
Saint Cloud, Minnesota

Dedicated
to
my children Andrew and Emily
through whom the heartstrings
of family and home, love and adventure
continue on...

ISBN: 0-87839-447-8
ISBN-13: 978-0-87839-447-0

First Edition, July 2011

Printed in the United States of America

Published by
North Star Press of St. Cloud, Inc.
P.O. Box 451
St. Cloud, Minnesota 56302

www.northstarpress.com
http://www.facebook.com/pages/North-Star-Press/100096141174

# LIST OF ILLUSTRATIONS

# TABLE OF CONTENTS

# HEART STRINGS

# EAST OF NOWHERE

## EAST OF NOWHERE

Still
Small voice
    of becoming,
    of belonging.

Settling through breezes
    soothing,
      whispering calmly,
        quietly.

East of nowhere –
    all along healing
      edges
    on inner landscapes
      of humanity.
Traces of heart
    and spirit resting
    on contented journeys
      toward home.

Treasured milestones
    and cherished
      landmarks
    for no longer
      wandering.
On comforting ledges
    east of nowhere.

September 2009 while camping solo at Sawbill Lake in the Boundary Waters

# BACK EAST RENEWAL

# Back East Renewal

Back East renewal –

Coming around through the years
        woven into homey patterns
        near to heart and down to earth.
Spaces and places.
Beyond and beneath
        compass point – E.
Marking new heartstrings
        and old connections,
        and deep yearnings of the spirit.

Back East –
A time honored image
        broadening charts
                and compass.
A welcoming place
        inspiring calm hearts
                and curious minds.
A varied space as vast
        as the inner landscape
                of humanity.

Back East –
        a well worn retreat
        of precise definition
                or vague location.
For meaningful memories
        along familiar streams
                of comfort.
For transforming perspectives
        on attitudes restoring

and grateful.
Beneath and beyond
renewal in all directions
east.

June 2010 as a companion to "Up North Reflections," "Down South Deflections" and "Out West Horizons"

# Vagabond Ventures

Undertow.
Underground.

Sing all around
        the world,
        and part way.

Back again.

Back home –
        vagabond
        on crooked boulevards.
Vacant.
Vintage wheels.

Colliding on roadways
        bumpy,
        and free.

Flying above ground.

July 2010 while hanging around in Duluth

# Passing Time

Wavy history
    happening
    in slow motion,
        beyond visual observation.

In water marks
    on rocks eternal –
    standing guard
        in solemn silence
        for who knows
            how long.
As sober imprints
    of time passing.

Passing time
    upon civilization
        re-entry,
        renewal.

In wilderness
    solitude.
In the company
    of a dear friend.

**August 2009 with writing help from Tom while paddling on Lake One in the Boundary Waters Canoe Area Wilderness**

# LAKESIDE  SUPRISE

Lakeside surprise,
  scenic anew.

Café Superior
  on the rise.
Delightful rustic class
   reinventing north shore
   old road vistas.

Along ragged contours
  of modernity,
  of motion
    slow.
And flash framed
   in waves rolling,
     reeling,
     crashing,
     careening.

In swirling patterns
  along ancient
    rhythms.
Always new,
  and scenic.

November 2010 at Scenic Café north of Duluth on Lake Superior

# MOVING  WALKWAY

Moving walkway
on fast steps
traveling.

Slower than the speed
of the world
rolling,
relentlessly.

In perpetual motion
waiting for no one,
for nothing.
As the furious race
promises to transform
relaxation,
restfully.

Into a healthy pace.

**November 2009 upon leaving the hospital**

# CROWS IN GOD'S ACRE

Crows –
    black and bold,
    stark and stoic,
        hanging out in God's Acre.

Flocking.
Squawking.
Cackling.
Messing with immortality.

A nuisance of noise
    in a peaceful
        place.
A bombardment of droppings
    in a sparkling
        space.
An unwelcome offering
    in the quiet midst
    of leaves scattering
        and gathering
        in an autumn harvest
          of beauty.

Crows in God's Acre.

October 2004 while staying in an old bed and breakfast inn across the street in historic Bethlehem, Pennsylvania

# QUEEN ANNE'S REVENGE

A murky mirage
    moving swiftly,
        silently –

Over the buffet table.
A bounty of southern foods
    lurking comfortably,
        complacently –

On Roanoke Island.
Blackbeard is back
    at restaurante
        Queen Anne's Revenge,
    bearing the infamous name
        of his ageless,
            timeless –

Pirate ship.

April 2006 with my brother Steve at a restaurant in Wanchese, North Carolina named for Blackbeard's pirate ship

# UNDERWAY AGAIN

Spirit of the Lowcountry
    on the water –
        again!!

In Charleston harbor
    after four decades
        absence.
Hardly pondered
    in wondering mind,
    nor longed for
        in wandering heart.

Underway.
Sunday sunshine
    and stack gas,
    and fluttering flocks
        of seagulls.

All the wounded way
    to Fort Sumter.

February 2011 on an excursion boat in the harbor in Charleston, South Carolina

# Little Sweepers

Sweepers.
Little boys
    chasing willies
        and wonders.

And each other.
In childhood search
    of merriment
        and magic.

And maybe order
    of a semblance
    unknown to adults.

Festive activities
    of little sweepers
    making proud –
        grandpa.

And the chief.

August 2008 while camping at Mt. Morris with Wesley and Jack

12

# RED HORIZON

A foamy summit.
Red Horizon
    of warmth.
On a chilly,
    gloomy,
      lonely evening.

In glorious Springtime
    at Gunflint Tavern
      window gazing,
      overlooking.

Big lake panorama
    of clearing calm
      arriving,
      unfolding.
From gusty showers
    and wild waves
      pounding on harbor jetty
      rocks.

Bearing dreamy promises.
Red horizon
    of dawn.

May 2010 at Gunflint Tavern in Grand Marais

# GRAFFITI  GHETTO

A wildly expressive
    not so secret
    counter-cultural life
        sprouting,
        flowering,
        bursting forth –

Conquering cozy boundaries
    of limited space
        and stifling convention.
In a graffiti ghetto
    more than taking over
    Victor's cuban café –
        extraordinary.

Revolutionary zeal
    and liberation attitudes
    coming to clumsy grips
        with colonialism.

Lingering in great food,
    Latin style
        and jazzy vibes.
All the mellow way
    south of contrary.

**March 2009 for Niki and crew at Victor's 1959 Café**

# CAPTAIN JACK

On a bumpy, twisting little road
      from Puerto Lindo to Cariari –
Through Costa Rican jungle terrain,
      bouncing through and around
        huge potholes,
        slower than slow.
Only twenty-two miles –
      yet an insufferable duration
        of over three hours
        in hotter than blazes,
           steamy tropical weather.

A journey in three distinct
      and very different stages:
        adventure,
        endurance,
        suffering.

With lively traveling companions
      led by Captain Jack –
        colorful character
          in high humor.

Promoting a spirit of adventure
      in stimulating conversation,
        storytelling entertainment
        and laughter galore.
Joyful hearts sinking
      in growing discomfort
        as endurance flared
        with burning sunshine
          and aching bodies.

And hurting spirits
    lapsed in sporadic visiting
    laced generously with complaints
       and even groans.
Unfolding in suffering –
    pure torture
       with silence reigning.

No one talked
    because no one needed
    words for expressing
       common thoughts.
And feelings
    on a similar wavelength
    of sharing together in suffering –
       waiting,
       hoping,
       longing.

For the welcome sight
    of the little town
       of Cariari.
Emerging from sultry haze
    of the jungle road
    with Jack by my side
       on a hard,
          narrow,
          weathered,
          wooden bench.

Sharing in suffering
    as well as endurance,
       and adventure!!

February 2010 finally – from a 1991 adventure with Nicaraguan friend Jack Kandler which could be sub-titled Sharing in Suffering

# DAILY GRIND

Daily Grind.
Unwind.

Coffee confusion,
       fusion,
       transfusion.

Transitions.
Transformations.

Rewind.
Caffeine on the mind:
       Morning Buzz.
       Jamaica Me Crazy.
       Shenandoah Blend.
       Tanzania Peaberry.
       Morning Of Life.

Unwind.
       from the daily grind.

May 2005 early in the morning hanging out in a coffee shop in Harrisonburg, Virginia

## WINTER WANING

Winter waning.
Like an old moon
      sinking slowly.

In morning sky
      brooding,
      brightening.

In pencil thin,
      wispy ribbons
         of pink.

Winter waning.
Like a new horizon
      crossing quickly.

February 2009 with hope on the horizon

18

# Nimble

Numbness
     settles in nimbly
     to dayliness,
        to ordinary.

In the midst
     of extraordinary
        events,
        situations,
        circumstances.

In the exhilaration
     of egos gone awry
        and slipping away.

Vanishing suddenly –
     like mist
     in hazy morning
        sunshine.

June 2008 playing around with words

# RELUCTANT SPRING

Spring.
Reluctantly arriving
    in slow motion
        swiftly.
And vanishing
    in a flash.

Spring.
Coldly circling
    through freezing
        rain.
And snow squalls
    in surprise.

Spring.
Reluctantly greening
    in steady time
        slowly.
And hardly budding
    through gray skies
    and sunshine drought.

Spring.
Reluctantly unfolding –
    finally!!

**May 2008 on permit day for a Spring canoe trip**

# DIFFICULT
# CROSSINGS

# CROSSING  BOUNDARIES

Crossing boundaries.

Living into new opportunities
    interesting,
    intriguing.
Challenging new perspectives
    of the heart.

Been down in the Village.
Been up in canoe country.
Been across the ocean
    for a broader slice
        of life.

More than geography.
Deeper than race
    and culture
    as differences
        don't need
        to divide.

Crossing boundaries.

January 2008 in a world too divided

# WHOLE  STORY

Always.
An understory
    to the unfolding
        of reality.

To drama.
When there's more
    to the picture
    than meets the eye –

Like it always does!!
Inevitably.
Naturally.

A compelling narrative
    lurking somewhere beneath
    the murky surface
        of what appears.

To be.
The whole story.
The real truth.

**February 2007 while attending a health care conference in downtown Minneapolis**

# DESERVING  BETTER

Deserving better
    than a haphazard,
        half-hearted.
Thoughtless effort
    to distort the sad truth,
    of an unwelcome,
        unceremonious departure.

A sneaky ambush.
A heartless execution.
Like a firing squad
    in the mistaken name
        of retirement.

Sanitized language
    for the sickening sake
    of putting smiles
        on the sad face
        of grim realities.

Downright dishonest
    and hypocritical.
Not really a retirement party –
    but a going away,
        a reluctant gathering
        for a fired employee.

Long appreciated
    and deeply valued
        by not merely me!!

November 2009 for longtime friend and co-worker Esther

# ACORNS

Acorns.
Strewn on the ground
    haphazardly,
    carelessly.
Work of a creature
    furry,
    fun loving.

Who knows beyond knowing
    instinctively,
    insightfully
        a new season
Unfolds.

Arriving not today
    yet soon enough
        for action.
And attention
    to natural signals
        embedded,
        existing.
Beyond time.

Beneath surface realities
    of acorns
    and squirrels.

September 2008 while watching squirrels at work

# DETOURS

Detours
>from reality
>on twisted roads
>>paved with deceptions,
>>littered with lies.

Too numerous to name.
Too devious to claim.

Detours
>from responsibility
>on slippery hillsides
>>lined with burdens,
>>heaped with denial.

Too heavy to face.
Too hurtful for grace.

**March 2007 from a hurtful place in my heart**

# TALKING HEADS

Avoid action
Join the conversation –
    media movement
        in endless circles.

Spinning the talk
    in do-nothing
        loops,
        lingo.
On the way nowhere
    positive nor productive.

Talking heads
    on liberal edges
        of public radio,
    on conservative ledges
        of boredom,
        of blabbering
            nonsense.
Shrill on sensitive egos.

Talking heads
    without listening ears
        in pop politics.
Sizzling in summertime
    media frenzy –
    like sharks feeding
        at intersections
        of entertainment glitz
           and issues.

Substantial and frivolous.

July 2009 on the sad state of media frenzy

# ISLE OF ICE

Isle of ice
    and barren rock –
        ancient,
        arctic attitude.
At sixty-four degrees
    north latitude.

Eyjafjallajokull.
Eruption volcanic
    shooting flames
        miles high,
    scorching lava fingers
        flowing,
    spreading ash plumes
        on westerly winds.

Exodus population
    in crippling wake
        of economic collapse.
Financial insolvency
    and personal disruption,
            devastation.

Deeper than natural
    disaster.

April 2010 reflections on troubles in Iceland

# Winter  of the Soul

Early morning light
    reveals
    a hush
    of new fallen
        snow.

Blanket of hope
    welcomes
    a new day.
At the crossroads
    of personal pain,
    of growing uncertainty
        and confusion.

Critical intersection
    of grief and opportunity,
    of loss and renewal
        and shaky hope.
In the midst
    of conflicting thoughts,
    of colliding feelings
        and bombarding realities.

In the winter
    of the soul.

February 2006 on the road in the midst of Midwestern winter of the soul as well as the landscape

# Asian Airflow

Monster quake
    and tsunami
    rocking Japan
        with incredible destruction
        and heartwrenching death.
To the foundations,
    and far into uncharted
        territory.

Nuclear disaster.
Unseen dangers
    lingering in aftermath
        of radiation.
Escaping.
Escalating catastrophe
    into private panic
        and public nightmare
        in a surreal daydream
           reality.

All too real
    and frightening.
Evacuating tens of thousands
    into safer zones,
        supposedly.

International alarm
    resounding,
    reverberating beyond denial
        into sobering action
        and historical reflection.

For a new, clear,
hopeful future.

March 2011with Japan in mind

## GASLIGHT REFLECTIONS

At the Gaslight.
Down in the Village.
On MacDougal Street
    with Dylan
    back in 62'.

Fifties fading
    in emerging folky days
    out of America
        and into the world.

A creative scene
    coming alive
    at murky coffee houses
        and smoky clubs.
On gritty urban streets.
All along Bleeker.
And around Washington Square –

artists strive
      giving expression
            to a new reality,
   music thrives
      and dreams unfold
      in a fresh wind
         blowing –

Bold.
Beautiful.
Full of promise.
Free of old constraints
      and new complaints
      at the bitter end
         of complacency.

May 2006 time traveling back to Greenwich Village in New York while reading Bob Dylan's
Chronicles, Volume 1

# TERESA'S  ON MULBERRY

Urban ambiance
  blowing
    on the gritty breeze
      of Canal Street.

On the outskirts
  of Chinatown –
      bustling commerce,
      teeming activity,
      roaring madcap traffic,
      blending languages
        into a global symphony.

Mingling sights and sounds,

and smells of cultural
    vitality.

And Mediterranean visions
    of calm days
        and charming nights.
At a cozy oasis
    of Little Italy –
        romance in the air
        at Teresa's on Mulberry.

June 1997 in wandering around in New York City

# Ask Patti

If you wonder
    about contrasting polarities,
    and enduring truth
        unfolding –

Ask Patti:
    can bleak
        be lovely?
    can stark
        be beautiful?

In shades of gray
    or black being burned.

A new definition
    of charming –
        CBGB style.
All the way back
    down on Bowery
    where punk
        bleeds peppermint.

And Patti prevails.
In the East Village
    all the helpless way
        forward.

April 2007 for poet, singer and songwriter Patti Smith ever new, always clear and compelling

# Waterfront Ruin

Waterfront ruin
    stretching endlessly,
        effortlessly,
    through changing moments
        and memories.

In dilapidated shades
    of decay:
        rainbow rust,
        metallic corrosion,
        wooden rot.
Asleep in splendid
    display:
        torn,
        tangled,
        tattered.

Ramshackle piers
    and abandoned ships
    listing toward murky
        graves.

Ghosts from glory days.

August 2005 while in Brooklyn

# INTERVIEW LIMA

Interview Lima –
Haunting tones
    of ghost ship
        echoing,
        resounding.
From long gone mists of time.
Scratchy voice
    of radio telephone
        emerging,
        reflecting.
Out of foggy memories fading.
From a helleva ride
    to Snowy Beach fleet operation
        off rugged coast
            of Maine.
Phantom ship
    struggling into howling
        gale winds of North Atlantic.
Surging wildly on boiling crests
    with wooden hull
        groaning,
        creaking,
        splintering away.
Crashing into foamy
    troughs of destruction
        and danger.
Lurking in giant waves
    giving way
    with a frightening
        lurch.
And blinding wall
    of sea spray

and ice.
Interview Lima –
Slipping unnoticed
into oblivion.

October 2010 reflecting on a wild ride back in 1972 on USS Observer (MSO-461)

# Vendue

Vendue Range
    in french quarter
        olde Charleston.

Near Cooper River
    flowing,
    following the stream
        of history.

Relentlessly.
Restlessly.
Through three stormy
    centuries –
        settlers,
        wars,
        hurricanes,
        pirates,
        politicians,
        slave traders.

Economies bustling
    and busting.
In deprivation
    and change,
    and restoration historic
        and human.

February 2011 in historic downtown Charleston

# LINES

Rounding rough edges
    and complicated corners
    along colored lines
        hardly clear.

In fuzzy focus
    on blurry horizons
        of fear.
Abiding safely
    within lines drawn
    on shattered landscapes
        of humanity.

Broken through time
    collapsing,
    colliding with history
        on the run.
Reeling precariously
    within rigid boundaries
        of shame.
In guilty patterns
    on ugly tapestries
        of racism.

Persisting insidiously
    within lines etched
    on wounded hearts
        and weary spirits.

**July 2010 while in the Boundary Waters reflecting on other boundaries**

# NOT  TO DREAM

Not to dream –
    a tragedy
    beyond imagination.

Hopes unknown,
    unfulfilled –
    dashed even before
        stirring
        in moments
        lost in time.

Failures unlearned,
    unborn –
    squashed ever after
        quivering
        in feelings
        captured by fear.

Not to dare –
    how dare you
        hold tightly
        to the flimsy reins
            of caution?

**August 1999 not sure where or why or whom**

# HISTORY IN THE WEAVING

History.
In the weaving.

Stories perceiving
      complex patterns,
      multi-layered textures
          through a lens.
Cracked and foggy.

Changing through time
      and place.
Rearranging realities
      along rough edges
      of years gone by,
          and still to come.

History.
In the weaving.

Insights receiving
      personal perspectives,
      political interpretations
          in interesting intersections
          of people and events.
Colliding.

August 2007 in preparation for a poetry reading at the Mocha Monkey Coffee Shop in Waconia

# BLOOMING  DAFFODILS

Daffodils blooming
    a bold yellow
       in sad commemoration
          of tragedy.

Long gone
    at Kent State.
Forty years
    and four students
    still dead in Ohio.
Precious young lives
    cut suddenly short
    in a shooting spree
       officially.

Nixon's tin soldiers
    firing real bullets
    in a National Guard
       nightmare.
Keeps on spinning
    against backdrop soundtrack
       of Neil Young
       and contextual music.

Forty years
    and four students
    still dead in Ohio.
And through history
    and blooming daffodils
       in Spring.

**May 2010 forty years down the trail from Kent State killings**

# MAKE COFFEE

Make coffee.
Not war
    in bitter grounds
        perking.

Always perking
    in greed
        far away.

And near at heart –
    always real
    in the home
        of insecurity.

Make coffee.
Not bedlam
    in sweet rounds
        steeping.

Always steeping
    in grandeur
        near at heart.

And far away –
    always real
    in the home
        of serenity.

**July 2009 in contemplation of a better way**

# LONG ROAD

Long road –
　　back to good vibrations
　　　　and desperado days.
Glowing in a golden
　　California sunset.

Eagles!!

Soaring on old currents
　　free flowing,
　　　　warmer than hell
　　　　　　freezing over.
With multi-layered moods
　　and complex patterns
　　　　of metaphors and meanings
　　　　　　mingling together.

On assisted living tour.

Palm trees
　　swaying desert breezes
　　　　of hotel california –
　　failing to leave
　　　　not an option.

On the long road
　　littered with broken dreams
　　　　and tattered horizons.
Stretching back yonder
　　to foggy beginnings
　　　　of hypocrisy.
And deception deeper

than a tequila sunrise.

All the lies
    buried in bloody sands
        of paradise fading.
In the cradle of civilization
    crumbling in financial collapse
        and ethical confusion,
    in senseless war
        and endless violence.

Spiraling along avenues
    etched in sorrow
    on the long road –
        home.

September 2008 with Norma at an Eagles "Long Road Out Of Eden" concert in downtown Minneapolis

# MAD  CITY AGAIN

Solidarity
    with Joe Hill,
    and the Wobblies
        on Capitol Square.

Mad City again.
Marching to rhythms
    of Woody and Pete
        and union blues.

In a new time
    of turmoil
    and struggle,
    and further diminishment
        of worker rights.
And value.

Solidarity
    with Wisconsin Fourteen,
    and public employees
        and teachers.

Mad City again.
In a blame game
    of blatant deception
        and lies.

February 2011 with Andrew in Madison, Wisconsin at Capitol Rally

# FUGITIVES

On the lam
     from fanatics
          rising.
On right wing agendas
     of wingnut
          proportions.

Fugitives
     for justice.
 On the run
     from futility
          sinking.

On selfish portfolios
     of nutcase sentiments.
Not so sweet
     slipping between cracks
          and crevices
          of humanity.

Regressing.

March 2011 for the Wisconsin Fourteen holding out in Illinois against union busters

# PRINCE OF LEOPOLIS

Prince of Leopolis
    lording it over
    a smaller than small
Collection
    of right-wing survivalists
        and gun nuts
        of every stripe
            except red.

Redneck haven
    tucked away in hillsides
        and remote valleys.
A polis of haphazard,
    ramshackle,
    run down buildings
        teetering on the edge
        of time standing still,
            and moving fast.

An explosive combination
    on old dusty,
    dirty rural crossroads,
        isolated more by choice
        than geography.

And history.

June 2006 from a very remote spot in central Wisconsin

# STILL  COLD

On a warm
    gloomy day
    in May –

It's still cold,
    chilly inside
    fortress walls.

And hardened hearts.

Like stone fences –
    rigid,
    immovable,
        dividing
        the countryside.

And conquering
    human spirits.

Like concrete buildings –
    ugly,
    faceless,
        cluttering
        urban landscapes.

Hope simmering
    slowly in May
        sunshine!!

May 2007 reflections on landscapes

# MIDNIGHT MUSIC

Drumming kettle
     shattering evening
          stillness.

Midnight music
     in frenzied patterns
     of unwelcome disarray,
          and aluminum urgency.

Wild whooping
     and frantic hollering
     in irregular rhythms,
          and amplified panic.

Across quiet wilderness
     waters.
Out of tune
     in simple design
     of chasing away
          marauding bears.

On the roam
     and in camp.

**September 2010 on Lake Two with Norma, and a bear in camp across the lake**

# HAMPTON  ROADS

Hampton Roads.

A water highway
     gleaming in golden
       sunshine.

Complicated in mazes
     of merchant traffic
     and greedy war
       commerce.

Profiteering center
     for pirates of Chesapeake
       sailing free
       of restraint.
And all constraints
     of modern convention
       and sensibility.

Hampton Roads.

Again –
     unlikely air arrival
     long after decades
       of absence.

July 2010 flying in to Norfolk, Virginia

# DIDJAKNOW

One word entrance
    to gossip city –

Didjaknow.

All syllables rolling
    together in mumbled
        crispness.
A poignant question
    without need
    of any punctuation
        markings.

Didjaknow.

A treasure hunt
    for juicy tidbits
    of personal information
        or speculation.
Like didjahear
    or didjasee –

Old norske words
    joining a lexicon
    of classy conversation
        starters.

May 2010 playing around with words

# ADRIFT

Feeling adrift
    on a rising wave
        of confusion.

And complexity.
Moving along haphazardly
    on a failure
        of comprehension,
        of pretension
            fading.
Into stormy days.

Feeling adrift
    on a melting floe
        of ice.

And sinking.
Moving along randomly
    on lake currents
        of disappointment,
        of disillusionment
            mounting.
On calm nights.

April 2007 while at Cove Point Lodge on the shore of Lake Superior

# CT SCAN

Talking machines
   snapping photos
      in efficient motion,
      inward journey.

Inhaling.
Exhaling.
Precious breath in captured
   moments of time
      standing still.
And moving forward
   toward an uncertain
      future.
Awaiting aneurysm status
   of CT Scan.

Machines talking
   in mellow tones
      soothing,
      signaling.

Activity.
Inactivity.
Blood flowing
   through vital arteries
   pulsing with oxygen.
And life enhancing
   health.

March 2010 while waiting at Methodist Hospital

## Scars

Scars.
Hide stories
    lurking within wounds
        waiting.

To be told.
To emerge from shadows
    into brightening light
        and new life.

Scars.
Give voice
    shaky and real
        wondering.

About meaning.
And mending hearts
    broken.

**March 2008 from an all too real place within**

# Not Amused

Not amused
>> with belated efforts
>>> half-hearted,
>>> foolhardy.

Finally coming clean,
>> telling the truth
>>> partially.
Bending around corners
>> of shaky interpretation.

Muse not.
Lost or found
>> in a raging storm
>>> of illness.
And foggy visions
>> searching ideas
>>> and insights.

Emerging from pathways
>> of creativity.

December 2009 not sure of context

# New Temptations

New species
   towering over landscapes
      of nature.

Blighted.
And bloated
   with progress
      running rampant
         in ugliness.

Unnatural.
Unnerving trees
   of cold steel
      and wire.
Undermining connections
   residing in humanity
      deeper than computers.

And cell phones.

New temptations
   rising over ridges
      of Fall Lake.

September 2010 in early days of cell tower controversy near the Boundary Waters Canoe
Area Wilderness

# CUT FACE CREEK

Cut Face Creek
    dribbling from highlands
    brow,
      blue sky smiling.

Wide with warmth
    and healing anew
    for old wounds
      brewing,
      bloody in time.

Returning through fragile
    memories tangled
      and torn.
Riddled with regrets
    and stifling reluctance
      to let go.
And weave new
    and creative patterns
    with fewer frowns.

Along Cut Face Creek
    bubbling over rocky cliffs
      ancient,
      scarred.

And crumbling.

**May 2010 on the north shore**

61

# GATHERING GRAYNESS

Dementia deepening.

Like an old photo –
    precious and fading,
      receding,
      retreating.

Into a fuzzy background
    of gathering grayness,
    of diminishing clarity
      and deepening darkness.

Darkness deepening.

Like a stormy night –
    lonely and frightening,
      retreating,
      receding.

Into a flashing tapestry
    of scattering colors,
    of expanding confusion
      and deepening dementia.

**March 2009 while at work**

# In Our Wrinkles

In our wrinkles.
Secrets hide –
      sheltered in shadows
         deepening
         with time.
Passing.
Lingering in moments
    of aging
        reluctantly.

In our wrinkles.
Stories reside –
      shared in wisdom
         broadening
         with perspective.
Growing.
Basking in moments
    of aging
        gracefully.

October 2008 reflecting on aging realities

# FUZZY MEMORIES

Pierce the darkness.
Point of light –
    tiny,
    telescoped,
    transcended by rainbow
       colors.

In fast forward
    motion.
Penetrating the spectrum
    of vision,
    of dreams only partially
       dreamed.
Yet to be realized.

Fuzzy memories
    fuel imagination,
    ignite inspiration
       in an ongoing search
       for fresh insight.

And enlightenment.
Flurry of hope –
    flooding in,
    flowing on,
    flushing out despair
       in perpetual motion.

June 2006 from too much time on the road and in the air, too much motion for too many years

# OLD ENOUGH

Inspiration sparks
    of creativity
        flowing free.
In spirit shining,
    soaring.

Bending imagination
    around new corners
        of vision.
And feeling.

Worry not.
About "being of your time"
    and "in your place."
For you cannot help
    but be your time.
And place –
    both helplessly fleeting
    and painfully brief.

Old enough
    to weather storms
        of a world.
Coming apart
    at fragile seams
        of cash.
And compassion
    left behind,
    along with too many
        people.

**May 2009 reflections on aging in a changing world**

# HEART
# STRINGS

# BEYOND BOUNDARIES

Paddling.
Border waters
    in wilderness beauty
        and wonder.

In all seasons
    of the soul,
    if not the calendar.

Fifty canoe trips
    flashing through time
        fading.
And aging realities
    and limitations
        dawning.

Camping.
Northern forests
    in wilderness calm
        and relaxation.

In a renewal
    of the heart.

**July 2010 on beginning my 50th boundary waters canoe trip**

# BEYOND  WORDS

Some trips
    transcend words –
    overcoming limitations
        of communication.

Journeys of the heart
    not really meant
        to be spoken,
    not intended
        to be translated.
Alphabet style:
    not reduced,
    not diminished,
    not confined
        to mere lines
            or rhyme.

Some trips
    simply are!!

June 2008 on being in the moment

# BAY BEACH

Bay Beach.
Old amusement park
      along rugged shoreline
          of Green Bay.

Bringing together
      generations of people –
          old and young.
In time collapsing
      in laps of fun,
          and grief.

Families intertwined
      by more than time
          and place.

Interconnected.
Interwoven well beyond
      simple comprehension
      and verbal communication.

In complex patterns
      of meaning.

June 2009 in Green Bay with family and friends at Bay Beach

# FLAM VALLEY

Running free
over mountain rock,
through forest wild.

Water moving,
flowing in timeless
connection
to all that dares
to endure.

Perpetual motion.
Pre-Cambrian foundation,
firmly grounded
in rock of ages.

June 2003 on the train crossing Norway to Oslo

# FJORD FARM

Aurland wanderings,
    wondering along
        a rocky way.

A simple hike,
    hillside confusion
        on a complex day.
Hospitality emerging,
    engaging personality
        at Bell Farm.

Paradise found
    in mountain beauty
    and fjord majesty.
A creative new vision
    in reflection and action,
    in stone and wood,
    in preservation and construction.

Philosophy unfolding.
Poetry unspoken.
Family history unknown,
    yet deeply rooted
        in past poverty
        and present Norway
            splendor.

Shining bright
    at fjord farm.

June 2003 on a countryside walk in fjord country

## FROM LAMBEAU TO LOMBARDI

From Lambeau to Lombardi –
Down through decades
    of football glories
        in Green Bay.
Home of origin.
Traditions transcending time,
    blending old triumphs
    with new dreams.
And opportunities to shine.

Born between golden eras
    with childhood stories
    of Grandpa and Curly
        playing rough tumble
        city team football.
Before they were Packers.
Coming of age
    with bike kid glories
    and Vince on the golf course
        caddying at Oneida.
Championship years defining
    autumn adventures
    in a shimmering sea
        of green and gold.
Youth section, row 2.

Half a lifetime gone –
    and now again
        at the Stadium.
With Andrew.
And statues bold
    and bronze

of Lambeau and Lombardi
larger than life.
Standing guard majestically
over stately traditions
deep and lingering,
and memories meandering
through time and place.
And hope.

November 2007 while at a Packer game with Andrew for an early 60th birthday present

# Door Connections

Rowley's Bay
    on Lake Michigan
        historic shoreline.

In Liberty Grove.
Northern Door County
    childhood connections
        mingling together.

In old patterns –
    always new,
    always comforting.
Transcending geography
    in lakeshore dining
        at Gill's Rock.
Overlooking waters
    calm and sparkling
        of death's door,
        of life's gateway.

On swirling currents –
    always wild
        and free.

**June 2009 while in Door County with Norma on a journey through the past**

# WORLD  SERIOUS

Autumn adventure –
    arriving automatically
        on the weeping winds
        of October.

Only two teams qualify
    following a long season
    marathon,
    surviving playoff magic
    after all –
National pastime pleasures
    sparkling like sunshine,
    splashing on golden leaves
        in misty moments
        before twilight turns
            shades of gray.

Into deep darkness.
World Series.
All for the love of baseball,
    glory – and money.

Or world serious?
A global panorama
    celebrating foggy dreams,
    unfolding behind tired eyes
        in mystery moments.

After dawn
    gives way reluctantly
        to gleaming daylight.

**October 2003 for Andrew my baseball buddy**

# Harvest Moon

Pumpkin picking
    moon –
        shining bright,
            and fuller
            than full.
Eye popping orange.

Riding east of everywhere.

Signaling harvest time
        in fields and forests,
        in coffee shops and cafes,
            and brew pubs.

West of nowhere.

Pumpkin craft beer
        and spice lattes,
        and good old fashioned
            pie with whipped cream.

Comfort delights
        for winter coming.

October 2007 enjoying a long, glorious autumn in Minnesota

# EL PASO AL CELIO

Stairway to heaven.
A culinary journey
       not simply an old song
       by Led Zeppelin –
           haunting,
           mysterious.
Long and rambling,
       belonging to ancient history.

Stairway to heaven
       lined with cornbread
       and tender string beans,
           sweet peppers,
           salsa pineapple.
And fried banana.

All the wonderful way
       to paradise.
All in a renovated
       classic cheese factory
       in dalles de Wisconsin.

October 2007 at the Cheese Factory Restaurant in Wisconsin Dells

# In Grooves

In grooves
    of creativity.
    flowing fluid.

In seams of activity,
    in longing for calm
        in the heart
        of bustling streets.

And quiet coffee shops
    and cozy cafes.
Connecting time and place
    with memory and meaning
    in complex patterns
        of clarity.

In grooves
    of comfort zones
    and consistency.

Nothing left to prove
    on bumpy pathways
    rolling along relentlessly,
        and restless.

No where left to move
    on smooth currents
    sailing along restfully,
        and resilient.

In grooves.

May 2009 for me as an author

# ReFiring

ReFiring –
    while still working
    within limitations
        defined –

Clearly.
And carefully
    with health enhancing,
    with mind expanding,
    with heart warming,
    with wellbeing empowering,
    with spirit lifting
        and life balancing.

ReBalancing.
ReFining
    while expecting less
    and giving more
        in simplicity.

ReFiring
    while slowly burning
    within crucibles
        contained –

In dreams soaring
    anew,
    and visions churning
        onward.

January 2008 on retiring and working as a both/and deal

# MANTRAS

Doing less
    with diminishing energy
    and shrinking resources.
Rather than the ridiculous,
    personally insulting,
    foolish new mantra
        promoting "more."

Doing more with less –
    a hypocrisy slogan.

More doing
    with decreasing focus
    and declining energy.
Rather than the sensible,
    personally respectful
    wise old mantra
        promoting "pace."

Doing less with more –
    a quality motto.

September 2009 playing with more than mere words

# HOMELAND NEVER SEEN

Through generations past
    and now long gone.

Woebegone feelings
    and soon to be
        experiences.
Tug gently
    at heart
    and soul.

Stories linger.
Memories diminish.
Names remain.
Locations change.

And dreams rise
    from ancestral mist
    in foggy longings
        for the homeland.

Never seen.

June 2003 on the way to Norway with Norma on our long awaited first trip to the old country

# HOMELAND  NOW SEEN

In the homeland
    now seen.

New visions forming
    through morning mist
        clearing.

Clarity emerging.
Understanding unfolding
    in fuzzy fragments.
New stories to tell.
Memories to cherish.

And fresh insights
    appearing through dim
        evening twilight.

Shining.

**July 2003 on the way home from Norway after our first trip to the old country**

# STREAM  REFLECTIONS

Stream reflections.

Autumn in the air,
        on the water.
Old swimming hole –
        clear pool bounded
                by flowing culvert
                and strewn stone damn.
Horizon blending
        in gentle banks bending,
        merging simple realities of rock,
                dirt and multi-colored leaves,
                placid sky and calm water.

Wedding weekend.

Shades of light and color
        dance through patterns of meaning.
Memories meander
        through time and place.
Generations gather at Mt. Morris
        and scatter again.
Clarity lingers and fades away
        in misty morning splendor.
Clouds in the water
        transfixed motion,
        transformed reality.

Stream reflections.

September 2003 from Dad's photograph taken at Mt. Morris on Andrew and Mary's wedding day

# CORNER  OF DREAMS

There is a corner –
>    not merely a bustling intersection
>        of urban activity,
>    but a critical crossroads
>        of heart and soul,
>        of relational experiences,
>            meaningful memories
>            and baseball history.

Michigan and Trumbull –
>    more than simple geography,
>        for real –
>        the gritty corktown corner home
>            of the Detroit Tigers.

Brilliant blue and green facade –
>    shimmering in bright autumn sunshine,
>    crumbling with the relentless
>        passage of time,
>    fading glory in magic
>        final game moments.

Gentle afternoon breezes –
>    blending timeless sounds and smells
>    into patterns of personal meaning
>        deeper than baseball
>        and well beyond time.

Here we are –
>    son and father together –

at the corner of dreams.
Slipping away
from one grand era
to another.
Hopefully!!

September 27, 1999 with Andrew at the very final major league baseball game played at
Tiger Stadium in Detroit

# COMERICA PARK

On the night
    soul came back
    to Detroit.

Dismal downtown.
Urban blight
    on rough edges
    of dazzling pockets
        of hope –
    lingering in the midst
        of hopelessness,
            depressing,
            dingy.

Four Tops rhythms
    rock old Motown
        to its roots.
Fireworks pierce
    the calm evening sky
        of Comerica Park.

Baseball buddies
    return to Detroit – twenty years
        from Corktown corner
        to Grand Circus Park.

All the way downtown –
    long gone
    and passed away
        in a glimmer.
A journey
    of heart
        and soul.

**June 2004 in the new ballpark of the Detroit Tigers**

# WRIGLEYVILLE

Windy City corner –
    of Clark and Addison,
    of history rich
        in urban tones.
And real in heartbeats
    of fans everywhere.

Wrigleyville.

Northside neighborhood
    of cubbie charm,
    of eternal hopes
        swiftly shattered –
In seasons of the soul
    throughout long years
    of torture and tragedy,
    and even a few glimpses
        of triumph.

April afternoon.
Snow flurries
    swirl in chilly air,
    separation of seventy years
        blend together.
In fathers and sons –
    four generations
    in the same ballpark.

Wrigleyville.

April 2005 with Andrew at my first baseball game at Wrigley field in Chicago where my
Dad first went with his Dad on the train from Green Bay back in 1932

## Baseball Boys

Miller Park
    outdoor baseball
        ambiance,
        adventure.

On site.
Opportunity to revisit
    place of origin
    for love of game
        and family.

From Bernie's Dugout
    to Tundra Territory.
From Dew Deck
    to Leinie Lodge,
    to field of green.
And precious memories
    paved in gold,
    embellished in time
    passing through years
        of aging.

Baseball boys
    carrying on traditions
        born of love.

May 2010 for grandsons Wesley and Jack while together at Miller Park in Milwaukee

# BUSTER TEST

The buster test –
    a humorous measure
      of alertness,
      of awakeness.

A frivolous,
    sudden,
      surprising shout:
        "hey buster!!"

A guaranteed smile
    if not hearty
      laughter –
    unless really sleeping
    or not paying attention.

Two boys standing
    bedside:
      "You're snoring, grandpa,"
        announced Jack.

"Not possible –
    I wasn't even sleeping."

"Yes you were,"
    declared Wesley.
    "We gave you
      the buster test
      and you didn't move."

Or even laugh!!

August 2010 a little foolishness for Wesley and Jack, and the original buster, my brother Al

# COZY HOME

Cozy home
    serenity,
    simplicity.

In caring hearts
    aflame.
In soaring spirits
    abloom.

Like Spring flowers
    brightening
    winter weary
        landscapes.

Cozy home.
No need to roam.

**May 2010 on being glad to stick around home**

# TROUBADOURS

Troubadours
    in the round –
      revolving along olden days
        turning,
          burning with soothing
            sounds.

In new St. Paul
    on riverfront summer
      evening,
      steaming.
Reprise re-union
    from Troubadour Club
    way back in LA –
      golden songs,
      nostalgia twinge.
Carole King.
James Taylor.
And original band
    with heartstring music
      for troubled friends
      and longtime lovers
        alike.

Alive with soul,
    spunky inspiration
  of fire and rain
    far away.
Yet drawing near –
    bound over yonder
    showering love and joy
      upon kindred spirits

Touching mellow strains
running too deep
to measure.

May 2010 with Norma at Excel Center in St. Paul for a concert by Carole King and James Taylor

# Opah!!

Eat Street.
Extraordinaire –

Christos
    on Nicollet,
    café cozy
        in multiple shades
        of blue and white.

Greek tavern music
    spreading joy,
    swirling through moods
        of celebration.

Soothing comfort food.
Tantalizing tastes
    of Greek isles.
Hospitality of the heart
    from Gus and Carol
    on the avenue
        twinkling bright
        with promise.

Sizzling saganaki
    and other cool dishes –
        Opah!!

November 2002 for Gus and Carol and all the good times and great food at Christos since opening month back in 1988

# MR. FISH

Beach art.
Colorful on pastel
     walls.

Outlining cheer
     in bold strokes
     of contentment.
At Mr. Fish
     in Myrtle Beach.

"You can't live on wishes.
   But you can live on fishes."

On King's Highway.
Black and bleu
     Mai Mai.

Bruised and uncomfortable –
   "like a fish
     wearing clothes."

February 2011 in Myrtle Beach, South Carolina

# ALWAYS CHANGING

Always changing.

Events swirling
    in a mix
      of churning people
        and places.

Happenings in moments
      cascading through chaos,
      moving along crooked
        pathways.

In search of solace
    and solitude,
    and wisdom
      in being.

Fully present.

February 2009 playing around with words

# McGOGLES

McGoogles.
Searching for connections
    and companionship
        more personal.

And real.
Than mouse clicking
    on the internet.

A neighborhood tavern
    transcending time and place
    with belonging beer,
    vino vitality,
        and giggles galore.

McGoogles –
    where all folks
        get better looking
        as nights roll on,
    where strangers
        don't mean danger,
    where green beers
        fuel more cheers.

McGoogles –
    where people
        are the real
            stars!!

March 2010 for a St. Paddy's Party at work

## SECLUDED CAMP

Secluded camp
    nestled,
        snuggled in forgotten
            finger bay
            of Lake Two.

Isolated.
Island dotted
        wilderness landscape
            of brooding rock
            and mixed pines.

Off the beaten track
        of canoe freeway.
        looming afar
            in the distance.
Paddlers battling wind
        and whitecaps
        along a horizon
            rolling.

And beckoning
        with challenges.

**September 2010 with Norma camping in the Fall at Lake Two**

## SWIRLING OTTERS

Swirling otters
    in twilight gray
        swooping,
        squeeking,
        sweeping.

In misty evening
    surprise –
        circling back,
        surging forth.
In effortless motion
    beyond carefulness
        and care.
In playfulness
    lacking purpose –
        perhaps.

Or so it seemed
    to happy campers
    being entertained
        in seclusion.

**September 2010 at secluded camp with Norma on Lake Two in the Boundary Waters**

# THE HILL

Notorious.
In canoe country
  lore.

The Insula hill
  lives large
  in portaging memory
    and sufferings.

No exaggeration –
  as the long climb
  and steep descent
    parallel the gorge
    cut through time
      and rock.

By Kawishiwi River.
Flowing free –
  winding through wilderness
  lakes and forests
  on a long journey
    twisting,
    turning.

Nowhere important
  in the wondering eyes
  of civilization culture.

July 2010 while camped deep into the wilderness at Insula Lake with Norma

# THE ROCK

Noted on map
    and memory –
        loosely.
A striking landmark
    in middle passage
    of Insula Lake.

Rugged rock face
    of historic awe,
    of temptation
        beckoning jumpers
        and thrill seekers.

Passing through canoe
    country.
Offering stunning wilderness
    vistas,
    visions of grandeur
        from on high.

Towering granite outcropping
    plunging thirty feet
    into cold depths
        of adventure.

July 2010 on Insula Lake scouting adventure a few decades after Norma's past jumping experiences

# MARION'S MERC

Marion's Merc –
    vintage 67'
    built like a tank.

Cruising through lanes
    narrow and winding,
    passing mountain valleys
        with wildflowers.

Blooming in rainbow colors.
Bursting in rear view
    vitality,
    valiant like Marion –
Living with cancer
    while dying from it
        gracefully,
        faithfully,
        joyfully.
In kindred spirit
    flowing,
    growing in love.

Marion's Merc –
    green torpedo dark
        and gleaming,
    fins flashing in sunlight
        bright.

Rocketing onward
    all the wounded way
        to glory.

September 2002 finally finished with fond memories of our dear friend Marion Troutman

# P<small>RECIOUS</small> M<small>OMENTS</small>

Strange.
Strain.
Rumbling
    through fringe
        fabrics.

Woven.
Weary.
Tumbling
    through torn,
        tatters.

Broken dreams.
Spoken visions
    of helpless longing,
        lingering.

In precious moments.
Arriving.

April 2005 while daydreaming during a meeting in Bethlehem, Pennsylvania

# THE KNITTERS

The knitters
>     gather gracefully,
>         peacefully –
> though not always quietly.

In the presence of Lake Superior
>     winter wonder land
>         of majestic vistas,
>         of ice and water –
> magic moments
>         of relaxation.

Stitching gentle threads
>     of more than yarn
>     into fabrics of function
>         and friendship.

In cherished spaces
>     woven between words
>         and quiet,
>     voice and listening,
>     reflection and solitude.

Letting go of busyness
>     and business.
Embracing creativity
>     and beauty.

The knitters gather
>     in simple patterns
>         of gratitude.

March 2006 for Norma and her knitting friends on a north shore getaway

# HURRICANE LOVE

Hurricane love.

Raging storm of calm
        and courage
                to be free.
Wild as the sea
        at Rodanthe.
Blowing through hearts
        of love –

At home.
        hibernating,
        awaiting snow
                in cozy log
                comfort –

Cuddled between
        vacation slipping away,
        and work beckoning
                like an unwelcome
                beacon of activity.

Arriving.

**January 2009 for Norma**

# Hope  Stars

Fire light.

Warming comfy home
in a soothing
recuperation
mood.

Dancing flames
flickering,
brightening.

Shining stars
with hope –

Hope stars.

Lighting circle windows
in an inspiring
display of simplicity.

Renewing spirit.

November 2009 from the homefront in going slow time

# HOLIDAY HEARTSTRINGS

Saxophone sadness
    tugging at lonely
    holiday heartstrings.

Hopes and fears
    of troubling,
        tumultuous years.
Merge –
    in melancholy notes
        moaning softly,
        rising triumphantly
        from an old sax
            bluesman.

A mellow weeping
    of tones bittersweet
        and precious,
        wounded
            and weary.

And warming
    holiday heartstrings.

December 2009 while listening to Kenny G at home recovering from surgeries

# DREAMWEAVING

Dreamweaving.

Adventures of longing hearts
    and wandering spirits.

In creative patterns
    of hopeful new
        possibilities.
Unfolding in discoveries
    unexpected,
        teeming with fresh
            opportunities.

Awaiting.
Awakening to relationships
    of growing trust,
        expanding understanding,
        deepening commitment,
        connecting communication,
        heightening mutuality,
        radiating joy,
        abounding hope.

And unconditional love
    expansive in spirit,
        extravagant in heart.

Dreamweaving.

April 2008 with Norma at Cove Point on the north shore

# East
# of
# Nowhere

# PLACES  OF THE HEART

East of lingering –

A peaceful contentment
      grounding emotional reality
      in visions
      of wonder
         and renewal.

Middle of mystery –

An accepting spirit
      calming places of the heart
      for journeys
      of restless
         homecoming.

January 2011 with hints of another book of poetry coming

# Xochimilco

Xochimilco –

Place of flowers
     along Bagley Street
          off 23$^{rd}$,
          on target
     of culinary delights.

And urban blight
     on ragged edges
     of Porter Street
          in mexican town.

Inner city destination –
     danger on breezes
     of decay swirling
          in the midst
          of renewal.

And hope rising.

February 2005 with friends Russ and Barb in Detroit

# TORTILLA FLAT

Tortilla Flat –
    spicing up
    downtown hill
        with comfort food
        and plenty of joy.

For all who dare
    to relax.
For fiesta!!

Dos Equis –
    amber brew flowing
    freely among friends.

Dos amigos
    arriving from afar –
        places west,
        and farther west.
In search of cerveza,
        comida,
        companionship.

And warm hospitality
    shared graciously
    by Benjamin
        and crew.

Tortilla Flat –
    cooling down
    uptown Bethlehem.

May 2006 for Steve – el otro amigo – on my last work trip east. Written large on the yellow wall in the back by the bano, although I heard Benjamin since closed up shop

# LAST TRIP TO BEDLAM

Resting.
On the peaceful eve
    of the last trip
        to bedlam.

Officially.
Legally.
Going out of office
    in a burst
        of inertia.

No regrets.
No hesitations.
No second thoughts
    or guilty feelings
    to lug along
        as baggage.
Bogging down
    or holding back.

Reflecting.
On the wounded edge
    of the very last
    of way too many
        trips to bedlam.

**June 2006 at the end of the line as a bureaucrat**

# USED  TO BE

Okay.

To be.
A used to be.
A has been
      on the rumpled circuit
      of living advancing,
          aging.

Declining.
Diminishing.
Not known –
      and happy
      to be unknown
          again.

And finally free!!

June 2009 on aging and changing and accepting new realities

# PIER  TANGO

Gray ghosts
  of Pier Tango
  swirling in misty
    limbo –

Captured
  between memories fading,
  and time long floating
    away.

In currents mysterious.
In vague observations
  lingering,
    looming on horizons
      fuzzy.

In concrete fog
  of once bustling
    naval activity.
Now resting quietly
  in haunting solitude
    of oblivion.

In old Charleston
  emerging anew,
  and ever scruffy.

February 2011 on the old Navy base in Charleston, South Carolina after an absence of 40 years

# CHUCKTOWN

Chucktown –
A lowcountry definition
    for highbrow history
        happening.

In imaginations
    free from reality.
Lured with fancy
    and fantasy
        combining.

In yarns bright
    and colorful –
        knitted together
            in new patterns.
Straining to stretch
    beyond a painful
    and tortured past.

Chucktown –
A lowcountry transformation
    of urban decay
        underway.

In upscale charm
    on downtown battery.
Longing for dignity,
    and simplicity
        connecting.

In stories inspiring

and compelling –
woven together
in old meanings.
Struggling to exist
beneath a hopeful
future.

February 2011 ode to Charleston, South Carolina many years down the road from slavery, reconstruction and legal segregation

# CRICKET SOUND

No reflection
    shimmering
    in murky waters.

Clear and cold.
Dim vision
    enfolding
    in darkening skies.

Brooding
    in cricket sound
    appearing overnight
      suddenly,
      surprisingly.

In a flash
    of autumn coming –
      unfolding.

Within summer yielding
    reluctantly,
    inevitably.

August 2009 reflections from home on changing seasons

# LAYERS  OF LOSS

Autumn leaves.
Flutter and fall
    through air crisp
        and clear.

Piling upon one another
    like layers of loss,
    like an old wool blanket.

Weighing down heavy
    and warm,
    and comforting.

Smothering old memories.
Weaving new stories.
    in complex patterns.

Complicated
In moments multi-layered
    like colored leaves
        beautiful,
        and decaying.

September 2007 while learning from friend Ted at a seminar in St. Paul

# TWILIGHT  DELIGHT

In sorrow and surprise –
   sadness arrives
   in feelings deep
     of heart.

Lingering.
Departing together.

In beginnings and endings –
   hope arises
   in fast fading
     twilight.

Delight.
Lost in darkening
   intensity,
   deeply feeling.
Evoking emotions
   strong
   and more than real.

In transforming personal pain
   into soothing music
   and inspiring art,
     touching souls
     with joy.

November 2008 enjoying a thought provoking twilight evening

# THE OLD  MUMBLER

A no show
    for the old
    folk singer.

No guitar playing.
No melody singing.
No small talking.

No direction home
    for the old
        mumbler.
Dylan rocked
    old St. Paul
        with heavy vibes.

And a new band.

Mumbling protest songs
    all along the watchtower,
    and through old history.

And way beyond.

October 2006 while at a Bob Dylan concert at Excel Center in St. Paul

# Pure White

Storm home.
On watch for howling
            winds of December.

Arriving in waves
            of blinding snow –
            pure white,
                        and falling steady.

Thick and heavy.

Winter arriving.
In furious blizzard gusts
            and bitter cold.
Swirling in drifts
            of falling snow –
            pure white,
                        and blinding sight.

Heavy and thick.

White Christmas
            in exhilarating beauty
                        and peacefulness.

Arriving suddenly.
Overtaking a long,
            lingering
                        autumn of melancholy
                                    starkness.

Breathtaking in splendor,
            and tragedy.

December 2009 as an indoors observer

## Morning Star

Superior sunrise
    skipping on lapping
        waves.

In ever changing colors
    blending pinks
        and oranges.
And rose reds
    in a mosaic
    of dancing light
        and intrigue.

Superior sunset
    splashing on quiet
        waters.

In ever changing colors
    blending reds
        and oranges.
And pastel pinks
    in a panorama
    of misty darkness
        and beauty.

Morning star
    shining bright
    on Superior dawn.

Misty.
And moody
    in Springtime season

stirring,
arriving.

Slower than slow.

April 2009 with Norma at Cove Point Lodge on Lake Superior

# KNOWBODY

DeRailed
>> from life activities
>>>> and world.

Action.
All political perspectives
>> merge in illness
>>>> and recovery.
And great food –
>> Cuban and Greek
>>>> Style.

DeTailed
>> for work obscurities
>>>> and oblivion.

Rest.
No professional directives
>> diverge in renewal
>>>> and illusion.
And mediocrity –
>> in an obvious
>>>> harmony.

DeConstructed.
When does a used-to-be
>> become a has-been
>> on the welcome way
>>>> to being.

A know-body.

April 2010 reflections on the obvious in light of aging and limitations

# SELF-PROPELLED

Self-propelled.
Slowly in motion
    along with water
        washing shorelines.

Clean of memory.

In stunning resistance
    to wind and waves,
        and steady paddling.

And untold agonies.
Propelled solo.
Gracefully in effort
    along with water
        moving onward.

Sparkling with promise.

In natural definition
    of hard work
        and progress.

Deeply satisfying.

July 2009 going solo in canoe country

# LOON-HEARTED

Paddle on . . .
    to places of welcome –
        sharing gifts and graces
        of compassion and hospitality,
          and adventure.

Loon-hearted friends
    bearing kindred spirits
        of freedom.
And magic songs
    of the wild
        within open hearts.

And all throughout
    the north country.

Paddle on . . .
    to spaces of serenity –
        experiencing graces and gifts
        of comfort and kindness,
          and relaxation.

Loon-hearted strangers
    bringing open hearts
        of longing.
And haunting voices
    of the ages
        to our spirits.

All along inner landscapes
    of humanity.

September 2010 for the fun of it all, and a little foolishness, too

130